Your little book can be really helpful.
But you have to help it

Congratulations - you're about to change your life!

Not overnight. Not without a lot of work. But you **can** change and you **will** change, if you try out what it says in your little book.

Note we said 'try'. That's the point about this approach when you're down or want to change – you need to work at changing things. This way, you learn a lot about what makes you tick, and the changes you make tend to stick.

But just reading the little book isn't enough.

You've got to read it over and over again, maybe scribble in the margins, and do a lot of other stuff that will help you get to the other side of your problem.

What kind of other stuff? Don't worry! You only have to do 15 things and one of them is putting the kettle on!

Are you ready for number 1?

THE TIME, THE PLACE, THE CHAIR, THE TEAPOT

Make a space for yourself

What you're doing is very important and you must treat it that way.

Choose a time and place each day to read your little book. It's your space, your time for changing.

Make it a quiet, comfy place, but not too luxurious. Sitting at a table is better than lounging on the settee, for instance. You're working on your life – don't slouch.

Put the kettle on and make a cup of tea to sip while you're working. And make sure you have two pens and a notebook or paper.

Two pens? So you don't have to stop if one runs out.

NO BOOZE, NO BISCUITS, NO IFS, NO BUTS

You need a clear head when you're changing your life

Some people say drinking helps them think. They're wrong. It clouds your judgement and fogs your brain.

Nibbling is also a distraction. If it's lunchtime, have lunch. Then go to your reading place and work on the book.

TV is something else you don't need, as is music. In fact, try to get rid of as much noise as possible in your reading place.

Shut the windows if there's traffic noise. Close the door if people are passing by. Switch off the TV, the radio, the PC and the phone.

THE
ZING
THING

Steal a trick from the movies

Just before they go in front of the camera, a lot of actors run on the spot for a few moments, or press hard against the wall, or trot up and down the stairs.

It gets them energised and adds an extra zing to their performance.

If you do the same before you sit down with your book each day, you'll feel livelier and more able to do what it suggests. You'll feel a bit more energetic and positive.

It doesn't really matter what you do, so long as it's something that uses your muscles.

You could do a few press-ups, touch your toes, jump up and down for a minute or so.

If your mobility isn't great, try pushing your hands together or stretching.

Number

4

READ IT 'TILL YOU KNOW IT BY HEART

If the book is falling apart, it probably means you aren't

Don't just read the book – **study it**.

Read every page carefully and think about what it's saying. Ask yourself "How does this apply to me?" Mark words that are important and write notes in the margin if this helps you remember what's being said.

At your reading sessions, you can read the whole book each time, or work with one or two pages. It doesn't matter which way you do it, just do it – again and again.

Your little book doesn't have many words for a good reason – so that you can read them over and over until you know them off by heart.

Oh, and don't worry if the book gets dog-eared and starts to fall apart – it means you're studying it the right way and probably making the changes you want to make.

READ IT
'TILL YOU
KNOW IT
BY
HEART

DON'T JUST SIT THERE, MAKE A PLAN!

It's not a reading book, it's a work book

When you've read and read your book and really know it, it's time to make a plan. Decide what you're going to do or change and work out how you'll do it.

Write your plan down, step by step. Be sure to make them small, simple steps that you will be able to do.

Use the Planner sheet on pages 14-15. You can download more for free from www.llttf.com.

Some of the books also have space for planning so be sure to write your notes and decisions on those pages. If there's no space in the book, use your paper and pens.

Remember, you're working on changing your life and your regular sessions are about making plans and checking progress, as well as reading the book.

DON'T JUST SIT THERE, MAKE A PLAN!

1. WHAT AM I GOING TO DO?

2. WHEN AM I GOING TO DO IT?

3. WHAT PROBLEMS OR DIFFICULTIES COULD ARISE, AND HOW CAN I OVERCOME THEM?

IS MY PLANNED TASK

Q. USEFUL FOR UNDERSTANDING
OR CHANGING HOW I AM?

YES ☐ NO ☐

Q. SPECIFIC, SO THAT I WILL
KNOW WHEN I HAVE DONE IT?

YES ☐ NO ☐

Q. REALISTIC, PRACTICAL
AND ACHIEVABLE?

YES ☐ NO ☐

MY NOTES

Number
6

THINK
ABOUT
ELEPHANTS

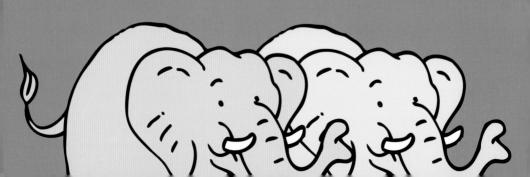

You can do anything if you break it into bits

How do you eat an elephant? In lots of little mouthfuls.

It's the same with changes to your life. Even if your task looks enormous, you **will** be able to do it if you break it into bits.

Let's say you want to cut down drinking. You could break the week into bits and just stop on Mondays, for example.

If you want to get out more, just work on part of the problem - like leaving the house or walking round the park.

Or if you're spending too much, you could start by just cutting out online shopping.

Most tasks can be chopped up like this, and you're much more likely to succeed when you do things bit by bit.

Number 7

WHAT IF YOU GET STUCK?

Don't worry, everyone does

Everybody gets stuck or discouraged. Nobody can sail straight through an important change in life without feeling fed up or going off the rails sometimes.

There are two things you must do about this:

1. Expect to get stuck from time to time

2. Work out what to do about it in advance

There are lots of things that can help you through the bad patches. Check the next few pages for ideas.

ACCEPT THAT THIS IS LIKE A NEW YEAR RESOLUTION

And you know what happens to them

We're all the same at New Year. Lots of good intentions, lots of plans to change our lives.

But then, often just a couple of weeks into January, we slip and go back to the bad old ways.

Here's what you do to stop your plan turning into a failed resolution:

Get a diary or your phone and mark the start of your plan.

Now, mark a Review Day on the same day every week for three months ahead.

Once a week, on every Review Day, think about how you're doing. Use the Review Sheet on pages 22-23 to plan your review.

Use the pattern of Plan, Do and Review to help you move forwards.

If you reckon you need more help, get in touch with your counsellor or supporter and ask for it. Or get more people to cheer for you.

Over the page is an idea that will help with this.

OK, HOW DID IT GO?

WHAT DID YOU PLAN TO DO?
WRITE IT HERE

DID YOU TRY TO DO IT?

YES   **NO**

IF YES:
1. WHAT WENT WELL?

2. WHAT DIDN'T GO SO WELL?

3. WHAT HAVE YOU LEARNED FROM WHAT HAPPENED?

4. HOW ARE YOU GOING TO APPLY WHAT YOU HAVE LEARNED?

IF NO: WHAT STOPPED YOU?

INTERNAL THINGS
(FORGOT, NOT ENOUGH TIME, PUT IT OFF, DIDN'T THINK I COULD DO IT, COULDN'T SEE THE POINT ETC.).

EXTERNAL THINGS
(OTHER PEOPLE, WORK OR HOME ISSUES ETC.).

HOW COULD YOU HAVE PLANNED TO TACKLE THESE THINGS?

GET YOUR FRIENDS AND FAMILY AND CARERS ON THE TEAM

Don't try and do this alone

The more people you involve in your project, the more likely it is to work out.

Right from the start, tell all the people you trust what you're doing and ask for their support. They'll be there for you when you slip, or when doubts set in. Phone them up and tell them how you feel.

If you have someone very close – a partner, husband, wife, best friend - you could even do your reading and planning sessions together. When you slip or get stuck, he or she will remind you why you're doing this and may even tell you things you don't want to hear.

That's what real friends are for.

SIT RIGHT DOWN AND WRITE YOURSELF A LETTER

Do it now, while you're all fired up

Imagine it's ten years from now and you're sitting down to write a thank you letter to yourself.

Life has changed and moved on. You want to thank the person you were ten years ago, for persevering, making the changes, sticking with things and keeping working on the future.

What would you write? Get your pen, turn the page and work it out.

Dear

I want to say thanks for being strong
ten years ago

Keep working on change
— stick in there
                Love from   Me

(Keep this letter and read it again
and again. It's your future. Don't
throw it away).

MAKE
A
NOTE

Remind yourself why you're doing all this

Pepper your fridge with post-it notes.

Write messages on them about why you want to change, what it will be like when you solve your problem, how great you're going to feel when it's done.

Now write some more and stick them in the bathroom, so you see them every morning. Write I CAN DO IT! in lipstick on the mirror (borrow some if you're a chap).

Stick notes on the kitchen cupboards, on the TV, on the steering wheel if you have a car and on your desk, tool bag, locker or PC. Arrange things so that your routine gets you face to face with at least ten messages each day.

And then, once a week, move them around so you don't get so used to seeing them you take no notice.

GIVE YOURSELF SOME GOOD ADVICE

What would you say to your best friend?

If you're feeling really stuck, this often works:

Imagine it's not you with the problem, but your best friend. He or she was doing really well but has struggled lately.

What would you say? How would you remind your friend that things will be great when the problem is sorted? How would you gently encourage him or her to get back on track?

Now say all that to yourself. Give yourself the advice and support that you'd give to your very best friend. You deserve it.

Number
13

THINK
LIKE
AN
ATHLETE

Get support wherever you can find it

Top athletes know they can't win alone. They look for a great coach and good advice and get help in every way they can.

You're just the same, so look around and get support from as many places as possible. It will help you stay on track and moving forward.

Accept help in any form whether it's face to face from a practitioner, by telephone, by email, via a reading group, treatment group, or from a voluntary sector worker or counsellor.

Like an athlete, you're aiming for a personal best. The more help you get, the more chance you have of making it.

MAKE YOUR SUPPORT SESSIONS COUNT

You're in charge, whoever you're talking to

Remember you're still in control whatever kind of supporter or practitioner you're talking to.

So don't just clam up or go 'um'. Instead, work out what you want to talk about an hour or so beforehand.

Maybe you're feeling stuck. Do you want to discuss a different problem? Are you having trouble finding time to make the most of your book? Have you made good progress and want to know what's next?

The best time to think about these things is before your session, not in the middle of a meeting, email or phone call.

Um...

YOU'VE GOT TO HAVE A REASON

It's sometimes easy to either forget or talk yourself out of getting the support you need from practitioners or other support workers. So, if you're seeing a worker or practitioner, at the end of every session make sure you both know why it's worth your while to have that next contact.

Whether it's face to face, telephone, or online support, there's got to be a good enough reason to make you want to go back.

- Something you want to understand more?

- A new skill you need advice on?

- Know you're needing ongoing support and encouragement?

- Or perhaps, someone to give you a push when you really need it.

That next appointment, follow up call or email could be the one that really helps make the difference to you and your life.

Use it, don't waste it.

'I'M ENJOYING THINGS AGAIN'

'I'M NOTICING A DIFFERENCE'

'IT'S HELPING ME MAKE CHANGES'

Number

15

TURN UP WITH AN WITH AN AGENDA

It will make your sessions really work

Even if you think about what you want to say beforehand, it's easy to forget when you're in the middle of a session, so write it down.

Write about your progress and how you're feeling. Make a note of the things you're finding hard, and what may be getting in the way. Write down what's going well and make a list of the things you've learned.

Remember, the life you're changing is yours. The project is yours and the project manager is you. So get your pen and write the agenda for each of your sessions.

What does an agenda look like? Turn the page, you'll find some blank agendas you can use.

AGENDA

FOR DISCUSSION DATED [   ]

WHAT'S GOING WELL? ....

....

....

WHAT'S NOT GOING SO WELL? ....

....

....

WHAT HAVE I LEARNED FROM THIS? ....

....

....

HOW AM I PUTTING WHAT I'VE LEARNED
INTO PRACTICE? ....

....

....

AGENDA

FOR DISCUSSION DATED [   ]

WHAT'S GOING WELL? ....
....
....

WHAT'S NOT GOING SO WELL? ....
....
....

WHAT HAVE I LEARNED FROM THIS? ....
....
....

HOW AM I PUTTING WHAT I'VE LEARNED
INTO PRACTICE? ....
....
....

HASSLE ME
HASSLE ME
HASSLE ME

It's easy to miss support sessions

Something comes up. Maybe you're too busy and forget. Or decide you can't be bothered. Or maybe you're feeling good - great - and that next support appointment doesn't feel like it's needed. Or maybe you've got a lot on and feel you don't have time for anything else, let alone a 20 minute session or phone call.

And so for times like these, it's useful to discuss in advance how much you want to be reminded, pestered or chased by your support worker.

A telephone call the next day, text or email might be helpful - or it could put you right off! You know what you're like, so talk about it and agree what would work best for you.

MORE THINGS THAT WILL HELP YOU HELP YOURSELF

This little book is a companion to all the ones on the right – it tells you how to get the most from each one.

You can get added help and support by working through the free linked online modules at www.llttf.com.

It also works with other self-help books – the ideas about planning and support are just the same.

When you've sorted your current problem, you might want to choose another little book and work on something else in your life. If so, don't forget you'll need this one as well, so hang on to it!